JU
19
the
tec ....ered anthroposophy in 1997, and began working as a member of staff at Rudolf Steiner House in Berlin, in addition to her architectural practice. In 2004 she received the stigmata, which transformed her life. Her first book, *And If He Has Not Been Raised...*, was published in German in 2005, and she now works principally as a lecturer and author. Several of her books are published in English, most recently *The Coronavirus Pandemic* (Temple Lodge 2020) and *Swan Wings* (Clairview 2021). She and her husband live in Berlin.

By the same author:

And If He Has Not Been Raised...
The Coronavirus Pandemic
Dementia
Descent into the Depths of the Earth
Illness and Healing
The Lord's Prayer
Secrets of the Stations of the Cross and the Grail Blood
Swan Wings, A Spiritual Autobiography

REINCARNATION AND KARMA

AN INTRODUCTION

The meaning of existence – from pre-birth plans to one's task in life

Judith von Halle

Translated by Frank Thomas Smith

CLAIRVIEW

Clairview Books
Russet, Sandy Lane
West Hoathly RH19 4QQ

www.clairviewbooks.com

Published in Great Britain by Clairview Books 2022

Originally published in German under the title *Reinkarnation und Karma, Eine einführung, Der Sinn des Daseins, Vom vorgeburtlichen Lebensplan zur individuellen Lebensaufgabe* by Verlag für Anthroposophie, Dornach, Switzerland 2021

A CIP catalogue record for this book is available from the British Library

ISBN 978 1 912992 37 9

Cover by Morgan Creative featuring *Ascent of the Blessed* by Hieronymus Bosch
Typeset by Symbiosys Technologies, Visakhapatnam, India
Printed and bound by 4Edge Ltd., Essex

CONTENTS

EDITOR'S FOREWORD

The meaning of life is *the* basic question of existence. It not only affects us in the course of an individual life, but also determines life within the social organism. The author is emphatic on this point, using an easily comprehensible train of thought in this lecture delivered to the general public.

The question of fate in the sense of career choice – which is particularly pressing in adolescence – is also connected to this basic question and subsequently, in a special way, the question of the meaning of *work*, which often arises dramatically in professional life – with the symptom of 'burnout' indicating its seriousness.

Was it indeed correct to choose a promising career, a 'rewarding' job, and not listen to the (perhaps quiet) voice of vocation? Where does 'vocation' actually come from? Where do 'innate' talents and abilities arise from? Is it merely the result of a gene-lottery, as scientifically explained, or a prenatal life plan? Does each person receive an individual life task, whether we are aware of it or not?

Countless reports of near-death experiences, with a review of one's life and an appearance of 'light' or the being of Christ, may be read as answers to such questions. Near-death experiences always have *one* result in common: afterwards, nothing is the same as it was before.

Faced with the finality of death, the dying person doesn't normally get a second chance. Even if he or she realizes what went wrong and what they now want to do

1

differently and better, death is apparently merciless. In such a situation one may seek a comforting answer in religion – which mostly offers 'eternal life' in heaven or hell.

But why should I bother with all this if I cannot continue what I started in life, successfully or not? Doesn't the idea of eternal life *without the possibility of development* indicate the meaninglessness of life as a one-time episode – often resulting in an egotistical, cynical attitude?

The redeeming answer is to be found in the idea of development – in the realization of reincarnation as a prerequisite for understanding one's own karma. The consciousness of the soul-core's immortality awakens: both before birth and after death.

After death, reconsideration of one's past life begins immediately (retrospection, repentance, intentions) – and before birth, preparation for the individual life plan, with the help of He whom Rudolf Steiner called the 'Lord of Karma'. The importance of freedom is increased decisively in the light of a Christian understanding of karma. To quote a later passage from this book:

> … [T]here are ways and means of gaining a conscious knowledge of the meaning of one's life today without waiting for death – without having to hope for a near-death experience. There are ways and means of achieving higher knowledge during earthly life – yes, it is our mission to do this. It is the reason God became human.

Joseph Morel, Verlag für Anthroposophie
Pentecost 2021

REINCARNATION AND KARMA

Lecture given to the general public on 11 November 2015

Until now I have been used to speaking to people who are familiar with anthroposophy* – in some cases people who have studied this philosophy for years, and who possess much more than a basic knowledge of the anthroposophical view of the human being. This evening the situation is different. This is a *public* lecture, directed to everyone interested in the subject, but with no previous deeper knowledge of anthroposophy. For this reason I ask for the understanding of those who may already be familiar with what will be said, and will therefore learn little that is new for them.

In my opinion, a previous special knowledge of reincarnation and karma is not at all necessary. In the course of how the subject is presented this evening, you will surely have the impression that everyone – on condition that they are objective – will be able easily to come to more than a 'belief' in reincarnation – namely, more of a *knowledge*, based on self-observation and insight, that something like a spiritual world exists, that rebirth is a reality and that, through a cycle of rebirths, the human being experiences karma, an individual path of destiny.

One can actually come to this conclusion on one's own, without having to accept outside knowledge or insights

---

*Anthroposophy is the name given to the spiritual philosophy founded by Rudolf Steiner (1861-1925).

based on faith alone. This is not hard, and I'm sure that you have already acquired a basic knowledge of the subject without anthroposophy. Possibly you have just not yet become so clearly aware of it. If we learn to observe a little more closely the manifold events of life that we encounter every day, and reflect upon them consciously in quiet moments, then we have already accomplished a sizable amount of anthroposophical work.

Probably all of us have questioned the meaning of life – probably the greatest, most meaningful question of all. I think it is correct that the question should be asked, and should not necessarily arise only out of a situation of despair.

Unfortunately, the present nature of our lives frequently diverts our attention from this basic question of existence, so that it is perhaps too little pursued to be answered to one's satisfaction. Or, it is raised only when one breaks down due to our present way of life, focused as it is on externals, or when a stroke of fate or a life crisis occurs.

Certainly, there is also an attitude in our society which results from a truly deep conviction in materialism, and which leads to an (apparent) superiority or condescension towards those who wonder whether human existence may extend beyond the limits of what is visible to the senses. Such thoughtful people are sometimes said to have an unstable psyche – or such questions are dismissed as a temporary consequence of a midlife crisis. This is seldom actually the case. But even if a psychological crisis were the trigger for one's question about the meaning of existence, one should be grateful for it. For with such a question we are touching on the basic conditions of our actions. We must then unavoidably ask ourselves why we do one thing or another in life. For our actions are in the most eminent sense connected with the question of the meaning of our existence.

Yes, it is a great question, and initially one certainly cannot answer it thoroughly. But – on a somewhat lower level – we might perhaps ask: 'Can I apply the question about the meaning of existence to myself, personally?' I could then reformulate the question: 'What is the meaning of *my* life? How does my life as such have meaning, a justification, and how can I give my life meaning?' Or: 'When do I actually experience my life as meaningful?'

One of the first important and fateful events in a person's life – a decision at a young age that leads to raising this question – is, as a rule, one's choice of career. At this point in one's biography – at the very latest – one asks: 'What do I really want to fill my life with – the whole span of my life that lies before me – in order for it to have meaning?'

This is a point in life when a person tries to orient themselves to something that can give them the prospect of meaningfulness in future life. They consider their interests, their individual capacities or talents. This is when it usually becomes clear in which direction they wish to go in order to experience life as meaningful. Well, perhaps some of you have, at some time or other, heard of people – or it might even be yourselves – who might say: 'Actually, I have no particular talents or abilities, I don't know what to do with myself. I don't sense a calling to some profession or other at all.' In my opinion this is a fatal illusion. Thank God it's an illusion! For the human being always has a task in life. We always have a purpose, a task to fulfil, as a member of the society.

5

To a considerable extent our current view of humanity and our concept of social status are also to blame when a person thinks this way. For example, in our culture a business manager or a medical doctor are generally regarded as superior, more 'valuable', than a baker or construction worker. But if we look at it from another point of view, if we consider the big picture of the human context, it quickly becomes apparent that this view is a gross misconception.

Just imagine – although this is a somewhat far-fetched example – that there were no bakers. Doctors would not be able to eat their supper, or would not have had breakfast in the morning and might be too weak to treat their patients properly. Or, our doctor might not even be able to get to their practice because nobody made the road that has to be taken in order to get to it. Through such a banal example, even a child can easily see that, within the entire social context, every person fulfils an indispensable task. In truth, nothing about the work of the construction worker is to be admired less than that of the doctor.

After all, it is not only an aptitude to perform certain fine motor movements, as in keyhole surgery, that is important, but also an aptitude or ability to perform a considerable amount of gruelling physical work, or to have the stamina to perform rather monotonous tasks, such as paving roads for hours or days, without running away before the job is actually completed! It's like in an orchestra: If all the musicians wanted to play the first violin, we could never hear a complete piano concerto.

We can call this orchestra, in which every individual being is active in the human community, a 'social organism'. Perhaps you have already heard this expression.

The word 'organism' is very appropriate, because instead of an orchestra we can think of a physical body with its almost infinite properties and functions. When we consider the physical body, we see that each organ has a specific function that cannot be taken over by any other organ. If the heart fails, its function cannot be taken over by the lungs, for example. If the liver fails, it's not sufficient that the kidneys continue to work.

And since every person within our human community is indispensable and irreplaceable, the expression 'social organism' seems quite appropriate to me. However, not everyone can consider this a fact – mostly because either they cannot understand or cannot find meaning in their lives, or they cannot find their 'special task'.

This is, of course, devastating, because it is not only a heavy burden to the individual, but also to the entire social organism, which must eventually fall ill – just as the physical organism does if an organ has to take on tasks for which it is not suited, or even when it fails completely. When such misunderstandings prevail, the entire human organism becomes ill. It is therefore not only absolutely necessary – on a personal level – that an individual finds the meaning and task of their life, but also for the vitality and health of humanity in general. This task does not necessarily have to be a 'professional' activity, as usually understood. I am talking about a *life task* that a person can feel if he or she examines their inner life – and this is not necessarily related to a conventional profession in the sense of 'a career'. Certainly this life task, this 'vocation', is very often related to a profession. But for the soul, it is not the outer activity which initially is in the foreground, but rather the inner feeling.

A person who has not yet found their life task may sense it when they do an activity that does *not* correspond to this life task. In our society, the activities of a person in their working life often clash with the unfulfilled feelings of their actual life task when – for whatever reason – they cannot carry this out.

When observing our sick social organism, one cannot avoid the fact that a largely materialistically-oriented perception of the meaning of life prevails. This materialism has brought a system of values with it within which the individual – that is his or her immortal, higher being – finds it quite difficult to unfold their (immortal) personality. Concepts of value dominate, which have very little to do with fulfilling a person's individual life task. You must be successful! If you are successful you will earn a lot of money! Being successful and earning money have obviously become synonymous. That is of course absurd, for fulfilling one's life task rarely has anything to do with earning a lot of money. Success in being able to carry out a life task, in feeling the meaning of life within the depths of one's soul through what one does, is an *ideal* and not a material matter.

So-called 'burnout' syndrome has become a widespread disease. Apparently, conditions must become extreme, even relating to health, before a person begins to realize that their exhaustion may not necessarily be due to overwork, but because they are not doing the work that they feel to be their personal task. Often it is only through such a crisis that this becomes clear. The realization comes: 'What I am doing is not for me. I only do it because I have not been given the opportunity to do something different, or because it is expected of me, or because I thought that the impressive financial rewards from such work would bring me fulfilment.'

This is a tragic development that is opposed to the individual human being. It goes against them and their life – against the realization of life, and even against the reality of life.

*

Although initially we have limited the theme of this lecture to an individual's daily work, this can provide an introduction to further aspects. When I was growing up – not so very long ago, although in fact over four decades ago – my parents had a *profession*. As a child I was asked: 'Which profession do you want to practice in later life?' Today that word is hardly used. Today it's called a *job*.

I am not concerned here with the creeping corruption of language, but rather that this change in terminology indicates a change in the perception of what an individual's work actually is. Whereas previously, when the word *profession* was used, it implied a kind of lifelong identification with the work corresponding to it, nowadays the word *job* implies detachment. A 'job' isn't necessarily something permanent. It can be changed quickly, indicating this or the other type of work.

A profession was more of a *vocation*; one felt called to a certain task. In the case of the unsteady job, the emphasis is often on earning enough money to keep one's head above water. You do your job in order to finance your survival. In this widespread view of what one spends a large part of one's life doing, there lies a biting cynicism – although it is not recognized as such. However, it is probably intuited. But today a step from feeling to recognition is required. The human individuality's existence and purpose is essentially

9

negated by this view of a person's professional life task. It is impossible to experience meaningfulness in this perception.

If work continues to be viewed in this way, an individual will feel that they are a slave to circumstances over which they have no control. A person will feel as if they are thrown into life, into a world whose laws they are unavoidably subject to. If they perceive their life in this way, it will be difficult to experience or achieve anything that is meaningful – to know the reason for one's existence in the world. A person will think: 'I work in order to earn money, and I *must* earn money to stay alive.' The satisfaction that one experiences through the fulfilment of true vocation is simply not possible.

An initiative such as Universal Basic Income* is based on the insights and efforts of Rudolf Steiner – the founder of anthroposophical spiritual science – in the sense that it systemically separates the concepts of *work* and *income*, which are currently fatally entangled. Instead of a person having to say, 'I work in order to earn money', in reality it should be: 'The social community provides me with sufficient income to pay for my living expenses and thus I am free to carry out work that I actually feel called to do, and through which I can pay back the social organism what it needs for its sustenance.' You can see that this approach is diametrically opposed to the principles of our current social and labour reality.

------

*Universal basic income is a sociopolitical financial transfer policy proposal in which all citizens of a given population regularly receive a legally stipulated and equal financial grant paid by the government without a means test. A basic income can be implemented nationally, regionally, or locally. (Wikipedia.)

According to Rudolf Steiner, a really significant part of personal karma depends on the separation of work and income, for the human being *wants to realize* his or her karmic intentions on earth. We want to experience directly the meaning of our existence. By means of what we can contribute through our individual talents and abilities, we want our work to be *useful* to the social organism. We want to be able to feel this! We want to feel the satisfaction that our work – which we do gladly because it carries out our individual biographical, karmic intentions – is needed and appreciated by the community. And in order to be able to realize these karmic intentions, we must be completely free – free from the psychic and physical burden of having to earn a living. If humanity could grasp this simple basic idea, the resulting changes in the world would immediately create space for a new conception of the human being as such, and of the *spiritual* meaning of our existence.

If humanity does not grasp this idea, access to feeling and knowledge of our true, namely spiritual, essence and developmental tasks, will be hindered. Whoever considers their 'job' as a punishment, as happens ever more frequently today – a job that must be endured silently until retirement, something to be got over with as soon as possible – will want to benumb themselves to the sense of the meaninglessness of such an existence. After work, that person may drink, take drugs or allow themselves to be consumed by television – or descend into the illusion of the parallel worlds of 'virtual reality', or so-called 'social networks', or flee into online forums or gaming communities – in which the true, living identities of the partners with whom they carry out dialogue is never revealed; where it is the norm to use an invented profile (or so-called 'avatar').

This process must and will end tragically, because the person is not willing to live within reality. What this means for the individual soul's life here on earth is illness, depression and insomnia – for in sleep, one is confronted with reality. There, the soul ascends to the spiritual regions of truth. Finally, one tries to suppress the unpleasant confrontation with truth by truncating dream-life and the experience of natural, deep sleep, through the effect of sleeping pills, which in turn leads to new psychical and physical illnesses. A vicious circle begins. If the karma that the soul had planned for itself cannot be realized, this is catastrophic – not only for the individual but also for the entire social organism.

I have dealt with this point in such detail in order to draw attention to a fundamental fact of life that affects every human being. The question of the meaning of life, of individual life – even if it is not always consciously expressed in this way – arrives with such tremendous force that ultimately it shapes decisively the existence of the global social organism. With regard to the present conditions of this social organism, we can say that the lack of perception, the inability to grasp a person's personal life task, perhaps indicate most clearly that this individual life task really exists – because it is by these social conditions that we measure whether we feel our life to be meaningful or not.

*

Now we can go a step further in our considerations. We can ask ourselves: 'Where in any case does this life task come from, and how does it actually come about? Who has "called" me to a certain profession to which I am drawn? And who or what has given me my individual talents, has

12

gifted me with certain abilities?' If we pay closer attention to this particular expression, we notice that a participle is used – that a verb is used here that is put into the passive tense. If one is gifted, one has been endowed with a gift.

Sometimes, when people are talking about the special talents of, for example, an artist, we hear the phase used that he or she 'brought that with him', or that he or she 'was born with it'. In this expression, probably used mostly without real thought, is a hint that can draw our attention to the question of reincarnation and karma. Thus, someone has brought a talent to their lives. That is, they have a talent for a certain activity, which they succeed in performing at a level that others cannot reach, even through strenuous practice. This ability didn't have to be acquired, it was just *there*, without it having particularly to be worked for. Such a talent is often apparent in early childhood. The person brings the desire for this activity with them, so that they also find practice easier, and progress quicker, than others.

There are two basic possibilities to try to determine where such a talent, where such a calling or vocation, actually comes from. The first possibility is that the answer is sought for in the material conditions of existence, i.e. that one directs one's search solely to what one perceives with the outer senses – or by a diversion with the help of technical means. The second possibility is to presuppose that something higher is inherent in the human being – we will leave this vague formulation for now – something higher that motivates us to ethical or selfless actions.

Which arguments and answers do those who look to the purely material world use? They will say, of course, that it comes from the genes! That a person brings one or more talents or specific interests into life due to a combination of one's genes. One must admit that, at the material level, this answer is quite correct. The genetic information of each person is completely individual – and in the future genes, or gene-mutations, will surely be discovered that can be identified as the source of certain naturally occurring talents. A combination results from the parents' gene-pool that is responsible, among other things, for naturally occurring abilities and interests that often become apparent in early childhood.

But every reasonably thoughtful person will not be satisfied with this assertion. We might ask: 'Why do *these* particular genes, which are combined from the large gene pool of my parents, constitute me with my talents, special interests and naturally predisposed longings?'

We receive an answer to this question from science that is actually *not* an answer. It is claimed that a 'gene lottery' is responsible for this combination. In other words, the human being is simply a random product of the fertilization process. The genes are combined arbitrarily and at random.

Well now, apart from the fact that – if the above were true – only an infinitely small probability exists that the genes could *always* arrange themselves into a *meaningful* structure (which they do) – i.e. one that can be identified as *human* and is so ingenious in its highly complex organization and astonishingly capable in its 'functional efficiency', that nothing even approximately comparable could be reproduced by humanity itself, let alone invented.

It is clear that the theory of the 'randomly produced' human being has not been thought through to the end. This thinking has made a mockery of the foundations of everyday human and interpersonal understanding, the foundations of ethics and the foundations of all social communities – and even the rule of law. Through this assertion, that we are a random product of the genetic lottery, the human being becomes *de facto* an 'un-I'. We are nothing more than an automaton. We would be remote-controlled, so to speak, by our genes, which we have neither chosen nor have under our control. We would be a marionette for evolution's whims.

Logically, however, this would mean that every moral authority would be rejected; that jurisdiction (laws in general) would have to be rewritten – at least the civil code and the penal code, but ultimately all codes. Jurisprudence would be abolished completely and the law books dispensed with altogether. A violent criminal could never be punished – after all, they are simply the slave of their genes, and would not be responsible for their actions, incapable of guilt. But the same would apply to the driver who recklessly parks their car in a no-parking zone and thus obstructs the loading of goods or pedestrian traffic. Where does one draw the line?

So you see, if we use the purely materialistic view of the world and of humanity to clarify the initial question of a person's vocation or natural gifts, at some point we come to a limit in this thinking. It cannot satisfactorily answer the question of where one's personal, individual being and talents come from, and nor can it explain one's sense of having a particular life task.

In truth, one's individual talents are not what directly constitutes one's vocation or task in life. They may make it easier to take up a certain profession in order to realize a task in life. But the life task can only manifest or reveal itself in the course of life. It may even lie in a completely different area than one's profession, and doesn't necessarily require a specific talent.

If we turn now to the second possibility of answering the question of where a talent comes from, this presupposes a higher, non-material being within the individual, that is, a 'soul-core'. Here, we not only find the answer to the question about individual talents, but also how someone with a task in life, but without any talents, can find fulfilment. There are many more people with a life task that is independent of their specific abilities, and thus of a 'favourable' genetic combination, than one may at first think.

Take an especially difficult or tragic destiny, such as a child's fatal illness. We may ask ourselves: 'What possibilities did the child have to turn its talents into a profession? It had certain aptitudes, but died before being able to use them. And is it even possible that it had a life task to realize?' Of course, in such destinies various aspects come into play. But often, in retrospect, it is possible to say: 'Yes, this child clearly had a life task – and fulfilled it. By means of its fatal illness and its dealing with this illness' – one often hears about how calm and composed fatally ill children are – 'it had the task of enabling its parents to have a different consciousness of life and death, and of what is essential in life.' What a great, self-sacrificing life task it is to lead two people to reflect on the true value of life! Many people with so-called disabilities often have the life task of awakening social competence in their caregivers, of forming affinity and helpfulness in them, simply through their existence.

Thus, if we use the second possibility to answer our initial question, one will come to see the human psychical or spiritual core of the human being as the source of his or her longings and motives for action.

But we have not yet explained where this individual life task – which we more or less strongly feel, sense or consciously recognize – actually comes from. As we have already said, it is strange that we feel it before we realize consciously that we have it – even though there are tragic cases – not uncommon – of people not even becoming aware of their life task. But one certainly suffers from the consequences of not fulfilling it.

The individual life task is there, whether we are aware of it or not, from the very beginning. But it cannot possibly come from the beginning of our lives, that is, from a time when we had no consciousness of ourselves, when we were still infants. Surely, we did not settle on our life plan – our challenges, our aspirations and our goals – as infants. Consequently, this means that our vocation, our life task, as well as our natural talents, must proceed from a context, from a time frame that lies *before* infancy. So we must look back to a *prenatal* existence. Yes, we must presuppose a prenatal existence of our actual soul-core before we can attempt to illuminate such a stage of existence.

Basically, these are totally rational processes of observation that indicate to us that we must once have existed in a state in which we did not inhabit a material, physical body. We must have been there before we 'incarnated'.

For many people today this idea is hard to grasp, for identification with the material body is so great that they experience themselves as united with it inseparably. To think that we also exist without this body – namely as *consciousness* of ourselves and our world – seems impossible. The idea is: 'If my body is gone, I, too, am gone.'

One could try to build a bridge to such a person who thinks like this by asking a question: If they were to lose all their limbs, would they consider themselves to be only half of what they were before, because half their body is missing – or would they still be the same person with the same *consciousness*, with the same ability to feel and so forth, despite the loss of their limbs? One would perhaps expect to hear from such a person with a materialistic – that is, a purely material – worldview of the sensory-perceptible world, that they would certainly believe they were still 'there', even if they had suffered the loss of parts of their physical body.

But one must reckon nevertheless with objections such as the following: As long as we have a head, we are still there – we are the same – because consciousness resides in the head. This can be observed in dementia, in which the brain deteriorates and the person 'disappears'. We often hear such arguments when we converse with people who are convinced by the current materialistic worldview. It is a deception, however, to believe that a person is no longer there once his or her brain deteriorates! Of course that person doesn't get lost or destroyed if their brain deteriorates. Their nature is truly that of a spiritual being who never 'disappears'. If the instrument of our earthly dwelling deteriorates, we are no longer able to use it as an instrument that is intact. The effects we achieve in the physical sensory world are of course different if the defective 'tools' of our body are no longer the same as they once were.

*

So let's assume that there *is* a prenatal existence – a state in which we *exist*, but without a physical body. Of what we know of ourselves here on earth, our 'being' remains – our thinking, feeling and impulses of will. So we would still be capable of all that, only we would not experience it within an enclosed body. We would therefore exist as a soul-core that is self-conscious and bodiless, but now perceiving a world filled with 'being'.

If what we described as a life task was indeed already present before infancy, it must have been defined and planned in this bodiless, prenatal existence. And since we were *conscious* – for we would never have lost our consciousness, but merely not yet taken on a physical body – it is credible that we were present during the creation of our future life task, and of the talents and prerequisites we would need for the fulfilment of this life task.

Could it even be that it was we ourselves who shaped all these conditions, which we would later feel so clearly to be our own in earthly life? Perhaps we had once known more about these circumstances and causes that shape our life on earth today, and we have forgotten them through being immersed in a body equipped with sensory organs and limbs for the material world, within which we are to implement our life's work – but which keeps us from remembering the prenatal states of consciousness?

With birth we – that is our conscious self – has immersed itself into the body with its limbs and sensory organs, and thus presumably was initially occupied with exploring the physical, sensory world. We would only gradually recollect our origin and our actual *self*, which is ultimately independent of the body.

And this reflection can start, as I said, when we sense – perhaps only vaguely at first, but later consciously – that we have been carrying around a life plan all along; that we are moving toward a goal, or at least are on a quest to know this goal, that is already recorded on the imaginary map we carry within us from the very beginning.

Let's leave this as a hypothesis for a moment and go a step further. We have entered this life on earth and are searching for our individual life task, because we feel this vague sensation about it, or our purpose. Maybe we'll find it, maybe we won't. But one day we will all arrive at the threshold we call 'the threshold of death'.

Let's now look at the opposite to the entry of our conscious self into a physical body – that is, the opposite of the prenatal state of our self's existence. We are not now looking at the prenatal but the postmortem state, beyond the threshold of death. What happens to us there?

That is of course a question people have been asking since time immemorial. In earlier times, people were wiser than now in respect to this subject. But it is possible to return to such wisdom, and at the same time retain what we have achieved in our development as human beings – which has allowed us to become independent of tribal life, priesthoods and royalty, and to become self-sufficient individuals. We might even make use of this wisdom we have gained for orientation in the spiritual world, in which of course we live without our bodily sensory organs.

If we ourselves have not yet had out-of-body experiences (in reality we have all had them, and have them all the time – only we aren't always conscious of them) then we might have a certain impression of what could await us beyond the threshold of death, according to the witness of countless people who have had so-called near-death experiences.

The systematic investigation of those witness accounts only began during the second half of the twentieth century. Thus it was only a relatively short time ago that interest in such experiences awoke. And it was only from that time on that it became possible for the people who had such experiences to report them without immediately being called dreamers or lunatics.

The American psychiatrist Dr Raymond A. Moody made the first compilation of statements* by people who were clinically dead – according to today's definition – for a certain period of time. These were statements about experiences that, according to medical assessment, could not have been experienced because of the fact that the bodily functions normally necessary for conscious experience and perception were no longer available. Many of these people would have permanently passed over the threshold of death and remained in the spiritual world had they not been brought back – that is, revived – by means of modern medicine . These circumstances have resulted in more and more people reporting perceptions and experiences they had in a state when their body – which often until then they had believed to be identical with themselves – could not offer them any possibilities for any kind of perception or conscious experience.

In fact, there are millions and millions of people the world over who have had such experiences. By now it is impossible even for the most hardened materialistic scientists to declare them all crazy – especially since the basic descriptions of these experiences are more-or-less identical. According to statistical research by the University of Berlin, in Germany alone over three-and-a-half million people are said to have had near-death experiences!

What will be of particular interest to us in respect to the theme of our lecture is the fact that almost all of those

---

*Raymond Moody, *Life After Life* (Mockingbird Books, 1975).

affected – regardless of their religious, social, ethnic, gender or age background, and regardless of the fact that the experiences are of course very individual in nature – report a flashback, a review of the life they have just led, which usually occurs directly after one crosses the threshold* and introduces the perceptions and experiences that follow.

This life's review or retrospective is unique in that it is undergone totally, one could almost say, 'super-personally'. The people concerned often describe it as like a three dimensional film of their whole life played with lightning speed – sometimes backward, sometimes forward – with all the details they had long forgotten and the feelings associated with the particular scenes, but also with the thoughts and impulses of will – not only their own, but also those of the other people involved. The events are experienced from one's own perspective as well as – and simultaneously – from the perspective of the other participants involved, which makes the review a means through which objectivity is experienced, instead of the usual personal viewpoint. The retrospective thus has a thoroughly moral component, but with those affected unanimously emphasizing that they never felt judged or condemned as a result. One's whole life is thus observed with a 'participative' objectivity – a selflessness.

For many people who have had this near-death experience – and it depends on how long a person remains in this intermediate region, and how long they are, externally considered, without consciousness – it also occurs

---

*The author is referring here to the 'threshold' between the physical and spiritual worlds.

that, subsequently, a higher entity appears, or that at some point the person becomes aware of this higher entity. It is often described as 'a figure of light' which, because of its living nature, is also the source of the light. This is 'light' in a redemptive, life-providing, illuminating and hopeful sense, giving confidence and positivity. At the same time, this is felt to be the epitome of love.

This love also enables people, in their bodiless state of consciousness, to reflect once again on what they have just seen, without intimidation or an oppressive sense of guilt, and then to ask themselves: 'What in my life, which I have just been able to observe again as a whole, was good and what was not so good?' This question is asked in relation to the criteria of light and love, that is, according to the moral principles of this high spiritual entity. The question becomes: 'Which of the many things or actions in my life was essential according to the objective criteria of love and light? And, which of them, according to the criteria of love and light (the truth), was meaningless or not beneficial? What was altruistic and what egoistic?'

The insight grows that not everything we consider good and right in our decisions and undertakings – or even ideas and judgments of certain situations or people during life on earth – is really good and right in the light of objective truth; in the light of love, which is selflessness. Those who have experienced such near-death often comment that people in earthly life are often deluded about this. With the supporting, sustaining and understanding presence of the spiritual entity, these reflections can thus be made by the soul without it breaking down emotionally. Its view of things becomes increasingly objective. It begins to view all events on earth in a completely different light – in the light of the high spirit entity. A totally new, much more comprehensive perspective results.

The soul realizes that as individuals, with our thoughts, feelings and actions, we are not only responsible for ourselves. Rather, that our actual purpose is to act, in our thoughts, feelings and actions, in such a way that we are beneficial to the community – for the great context of all beings. We realize that, directly or indirectly, our thoughts, feelings and actions always affects this context. The individual is not only responsible – this is how those who have undergone near-death experiences describe it – for caring for oneself, being honest with oneself, and so forth. It is also our responsibility to act in that way because our inner life – which until then we had always considered to be private – is in reality also important for all humanity, and in fact just as important for ourselves. We recognize now, beyond the threshold of death, that everything we have done, thought and felt, has resonance not only for our own – imperishable – spirit-being, but also for the whole world, our fellow humans, the animals, and for the earth.

It becomes ever clearer to the individual soul in this situation that it bears the inner wish to give something to this earth organism of which we are a part; that it wants to wipe off, like a dusty covering, the old, prevailing feeling in earthly life that always wants something *from* the world.

Thus, the question of one's *life task* comes to the fore.

*

I have already mentioned the near-death researcher Dr Moody. His first book included the striking near-death experience of a young soldier in the US Army, George Ritchie. In George Ritchie's own book, *Return From Tomorrow*, he reports on an experience very similar to the one

I have just sketched out. With his life review in the background, he describes his experience of being asked by the being that radiated light and love, whom he identifies as Christ: '*What have you done with your life?*' The then 19-year-old, who had so far led an average life with average motives and goals (such as attending a good university or earning a Boy Scouts' badge of merit) was forced to realize that, until then, he had thought or achieved hardly anything of real significance that could have constituted merit in the light of truth and love. This realization came to him in the presence of the loving, sympathetic light.

It was the entity of light's loving concern to make him aware that he could still give deeper meaning to his life (which of course was not yet at an end); that he could give something to the world, and that he should still make something of his life – so that one day he could return to this point beyond the threshold of death, and give a different answer to that same question. In the future, when reviewing his completed life, he would then be able to say that whilst he had not always done everything correctly, he had made an effort and certainly did achieve something! His life would therefore have had a meaning for the world (and therefore also for himself)!*

The characteristic of near-death experiences is that the people who have them do not remain in the spiritual world, but return to their earthly lives within seconds or minutes. They don't 'definitively' die, which is why we speak of *near*-death experiences. They get a second chance, so to speak, to restart their lives according to truly meaningful perspectives. And it is almost always

---

*See Appendix 2 for quotation and fuller context.

told that the person concerned does not return to their old life – that is, no longer continues to do everything in the same way as before, but begins to live according to a completely new criteria of values. The person becomes much more alert and discreet, detests conflict and violence, everyday agitation and selfish ambition. Mostly, they choose an 'occupation' in which they begin to act, in a more-or-less noticeable way, according to higher – what we might call 'divine' – principles, which the person learned to know and esteem in their bodiless state. They know that the world will only progress if it is organized according to such principles. The inner, impersonal and thus selfless wish of these people is to consider every human being as loved by the entity of light and love, and for them to give something wholesome and beneficial to the fraternal community of humanity.

But not everyone experiences such a wake-up call, and not everyone has a near-death experience in life. And not everyone is familiar with the relevant literature. Some people are able to view their lives self-critically when facing death, in old age or when affected by a terminal illness. Then questions may arise that were not asked previously, and are similar in nature to the question of conscience that the divine entity asked George Ritchie. Standing directly before the threshold of death, the individual may suddenly ask themselves: 'Have I actually done everything right in my life, and did I achieve what I could have achieved?' Or rather: 'Have I actually made an effort to progress myself in a way that is lasting and that really counts?' And then, as often happens, the person admits: 'Oh, if only I had more time! I would now do many things differently!' But by then it's too late…

What do such people feel when standing before the threshold of death? What can give them solace, hope and perspective? What can they turn to? Perhaps initially to their religion – to the religious institution to which they belong and, in such situations, that they suddenly remember! And they ask themselves: 'What does my religion's teaching say about this dilemma? What does it say about what awaits me after death?'

And here we must realize that it is not only the Jewish or the Islamic religions, but also the Christian denominations – which traditionally predominate in Europe – that teach their faithful something about 'eternal life'. This 'eternal life', however, is in no way understood as was originally meant when, according to the testimonies of the evangelists, Christ Jesus spoke about an 'eternal life'. Christian teaching interprets these words today as though they refer to an eternal life after death. Thus, the soul will 'resurrect' – it will overcome death after the body's death and then live eternally, without a body, in the spiritual world – if the person had behaved properly in earthly life. If not, at worst an eternal existence awaits them in hell. Either way, one is faced with an eternal life as a soul without a body, in a purely spiritual world – a beautiful or a terrible spiritual world.

In actual fact, however, the main Christian denominations lack the all-important principle of development in their teachings! And it is exactly this principle of development which will be emphasized in this evening's considerations. Please don't misunderstand me. I don't mean that Christianity or the Christ-Mystery lack the principle of development! I refer, rather, to the current (popular) interpretation of the holy scriptures. In case you are not intimately familiar with the New Testament, you may be astonished to hear that there are passages in it that indicate clearly that the individual human soul does not only live *once* on earth.

Knowledge of reincarnation was so self-evident in those times that when the Lord asked his disciples who the people thought He was, they answered, matter-of-factly: 'Some say John the Baptist, but others Elijah, still others Jeremiah or one of the prophets' (Matt. 16:14). Also, the Pharisees asked John the Baptist directly about his previous incarnation (John 1:21), and the Christ Jesus himself told his disciples: 'Yes, he is Elijah, who is to come again' (Matt. 11:14).

The concept of repeated earth lives was so self-evident at that time that the evangelists did not consider it necessary to elaborate. It is something of a casual reference. On the other hand, there is no mention that the development of the human soul is cancelled by the appearance of God on earth or by His sacrificial act. Therefore, 'eternal life' does not refer to an unending existence in *nirvana* – in the kingdom of heaven – but rather to the fact that the soul no longer loses consciousness after it has discarded the physical body.

This new aspect of the human soul's evolution is related to the fact that Christ is the 'dispenser' of the Holy Spirit. This means that the consciousness of the individual human soul is ignited. A new era dawns, which gradually leads the human being from, so to speak, the immature stage of group-consciousness to individual consciousness. This doesn't mean the soul's self-consciousness. Human beings had that already two or three thousand years ago. What it means is that human beings are also able to become independent in their *spiritual* consciousness. Previously, they couldn't find their own conscious connection to divine wisdom, but were dependent on the spiritual authority of a priest, an initiate, or someone to lead them that was chosen by a higher authority. And this spiritual consciousness was now to stay with them after death. By realizing that they possessed an immortal soul, they became truly immortal. They could become conscious of their immortality – the immortality of their soul-core, their 'I'.

Thus, during their lives on earth, human beings became able to build and maintain an intimate spiritual relationship with the spiritual world. Human beings were now accompanied by the 'advocate' (John 16:7) – as Christ also called the Holy Spirit – the Spirit of Truth. People could now understand higher moral principles as an aid for developing their souls, and therefore no longer needed high priests to prescribe a moral code for them to follow, without understanding why.

Whoever has a spirit can now undertake responsibility, in a higher sense, for themselves and for the world in which they live.

This (old) understanding of 'eternal life', which is the opposite of the 'second death' mentioned in John's Revelation – namely *spiritual* death – was maintained by the Christian Church for several centuries. Of course, the Church knew the secret principle of development of spiritually-knowledgeable souls, as initiated by Christ, and it knew about the new spiritual maturity that *every* person could develop – a fact which, however, was not compatible with the institutional claims to power of later ecclesiastical dignitaries, which is why it was unceremoniously removed from the doctrine of the Roman Catholic Church by means of dogma. Since then, the faithful person who asks about existence after death is taught the doctrine of 'eternal life' in God's kingdom of heaven or, alternatively, of eternal burning in hell – depending on whether one is deemed worthy to take up eternal residence in the kingdom of heaven by the great one who 'weighs' souls.

But if the true believer were to take a closer look at the requirements that need to be met in order to have eternal abode in heaven, he or she will realize inevitably that there would hardly be a handful of souls in the entire history of humanity who were able to satisfy fully these requirements during their life on earth. No matter how good a Christian we may be, and how much we may have tried to make Christian principles our ideals, on honest self-examination we will have to admit that we have repeatedly abandoned these principles, and that ultimately we have not been able to achieve these high ethical ideals in life.

What does that mean? We may say to ourselves: 'Why should I exert myself? The goal is unattainable. In such a short life I simply cannot do it. Life makes no sense this way. Why does one even live? What, and above all why, should one achieve something here?'

There are actually only two alternatives at this point. Either one becomes an atheist and is content with the idea of *nothing* after death – that is, the concept of life as a one-time episode (which, incidentally, is not much different from the idea that, after a single life, one goes directly – and remains eternally – in heaven or hell). Then one might become a cynic and a convinced egotist. Or, one uses the spiritual tools that Christ gave us and takes up a path of knowledge in order to find out what existence after death is really like.

This is where we paused earlier. By careful observation and common sense, a strong bridge can be built to insights into real conditions, for they reveal themselves through all that happens here on earth.

Each person, whether an atheist or with religious convictions, has a natural aspiration for their existence: we want to give our life meaning; we want to set goals for ourselves, to have ideals. And, as a rule, we are willing to submit to the laws of a (political) state – based on its understanding of good and evil, right and wrong – which exist in order to protect good from evil and right from wrong.

Even the atheist will become depressive, aggressive, dully obtuse or physically ill, if he or she does not live life as an individual 'I'. That's why the atheist also has an inner compass, which is based in his or her spiritual core (no matter how much they may deny it). In *every* human being there is a higher entity to which he or she can connect consciously. This entity gives each of us the ability to develop a conscience, an awareness of responsibility, commitment, compassion, a willing to sacrifice, a sense of justice... Every person contains within them the seed of will to fulfil their life with meaning. We feel vaguely or more clearly: 'There is something that drives me to achieve this or the other thing, to experience this or the other thing. In other words, there is a guideline or plan to my life – even if I don't consciously recognize it or cannot implement it.'

Every reasonably attentive person, listening to his or her inner self, or even listening to the outer world, will ask themselves how they are to fulfil their life with meaning, so long as the meaning of human existence remains unknown to them. They will come to the point in these deliberations where they say to themselves what I mentioned earlier:

'What constitutes me as a singular human being, my individual abilities – also my deficiencies and my inclinations, which are naturally my own – must originate from a context that reaches back before birth, for these traits already existed at birth. So, they must have been arranged as integral parts of a larger plan for my individual being, within a framework in which as yet I had no physical body.'

However, one usually only finds what we have called a life task after a number of years into life, and the great learning process only truly begins once it has been grasped. But one day we will come to the end of our life on earth and, looking back, say to ourselves: 'Yes, even though I was lucky enough to have gone through a learning process, why is it that I am only now somewhat wiser, at the end of my life, when I can no longer use these insights?'

Only those who have experienced near-death are given that (second) chance. For them, the question as to whether they have used their lifetime meaningfully arises mostly towards the beginning or in the middle of their conscious life, because of that event in their destiny. They still have time to let higher knowledge flow into life and to change accordingly. But most people will be confronted with this question, and the resulting insights, only after their 'definitive' crossing over the threshold of death.

So then, what is the point of a prenatal plan for life and a postmortem review? What are they for, especially if we assume that life on earth is a singular affair?

When you think about these things, you are already on the correct path to knowledge. For there is actually only one coherent conclusion to be drawn. The whole concept of human existence makes no sense if you believe the materialistic (ultimately, atheistic) worldview, or if you believe the Church's doctrine that you only live *once*. Then – and only then – does the concept of human existence make no sense. It makes no sense so long as we assign development solely to the human species as a whole and not to the individuality. The development of individuality cannot be provided for in *one* lifetime – certainly not under the very different living conditions into which people are born.

Everything indicates that reincarnation is a reality for the individual human spirit – that there are repeated lives on earth! Let's consider this with a sketch:

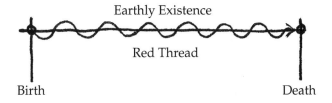

Earthly Existence

Red Thread

Birth   Death

Figure 1

So we have – and this is probably indisputable – the span of our earthly existence, our earthly life, which extends between the beginning and end points of birth and death. Within this span of life, we can sense a kind of life task, a life plan. It runs through our earthly life like a red thread.

Now, we have established that the thread doesn't begin at birth, but extends beyond this point of birth, that is, back into the prenatal, namely spiritual existence [see 'A' in Fig. 2]. And it doesn't end at death, but also extends beyond this endpoint into after-death existence ['B'], where the implementation of the plan awaits us.

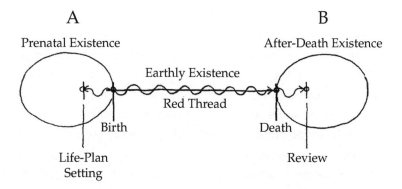

Figure 2

We can now see that spheres 'A' and 'B' are identical. The red thread that runs through our earthly life begins and ends in the same sphere: in the spiritual world. In this spiritual world, work is prepared (namely, before birth) and then afterward (namely, after death) is realized. But both are close together.

When we cross the threshold of physical death, we don't enter into nothingness. Nor do we arrive at heaven or hell and remain there for eternity! Instead, we are involved in great activity. For in that sphere – the spiritual world – we are occupied with conscious preparation for our next incarnation, as well as the conscious evaluation of this incarnation. During the evaluation process, our merits, as well as our deficiencies or vices, are shown in the light of truth. We do not meet a punishing God. Rather, we experience – as those who have had near-death experiences testify – the consequences of our own behaviour as self-reliant human beings, in the context of the spiritual world's reality, the principles of which are selflessness and love.

If you read George Ritchie's description of his near-death experience, you will find a scene in which it is confirmed that it is not God who banishes us from the peace of light and love, but it is we ourselves, if we do not (at least attempt) to free ourselves from our vices. In his book, the postmortem souls of drinkers are described, who cannot satisfy their addiction because they no longer have physical bodies. It is clear by this rather extreme example that one isn't simply rid of bad habits after death, if one hasn't already freed oneself from them during earthly life. Rather, one can experience a kind of 'hell' in after-death existence if these bad habits were of an extreme nature. The soul desires something – it longs for something that can only be satisfied in a physical-material body, which, however, has already been discarded. What is desired must eventually be overcome.

When we complete our review in the postmortem sphere and, with full consciousness and objectively, confront what we have done, thought and felt – and what consequences this has in the overall context of cosmic existence of the world and human organism – at some point we will feel that one thing or another in our lives was false. We regret it, and would gladly make up for it. But that's not possible. It's too late! Our body has been discarded. We have 'died'.

This is the point where it becomes clear to the soul how its life plan originated, from where the life task – that one always felt subliminally – actually proceeds from, and why one had certain talents and certain weaknesses from birth onwards. The soul senses: 'Here, in the review of my past life, lies the root of my new life plan! My consciousness did not die with my body's death. On the contrary.'

35

Rather, my (disembodied) self has recognized that my life plan must have been the result of an earlier, previous life; because now that my life is over and I look back at my achievements, my newly acquired skills and insights – which I can no longer make use of – as well as my failures and errors, I begin to realize and wish that someday I will have another life on earth. In this new life I would be able to deploy insights and abilities I acquired in my life that just ended. They should be of benefit to the world! And the omissions and errors should also be compensated for, which now I recognize as such, in the light of the living truth. So the soul tells itself after death. Thus it resolves to begin a new life.

In this way, it can become clear to us who, actually, gave us our life task. It was ourselves! Our immortal core of being, our spiritual consciousness – with the help of higher spiritual entities or beings – conceived our life plan in the prenatal sphere, and prepared it through the results of a previous life. It is our actual 'I' that goes on living 'eternally' from one incarnation to the next, in order to *develop* ever more beneficently.

What we also call *karma* is co-created in freedom and knowledge by our own core of being! This life plan has been designed so perfectly by wise spirits, by the Christ, the 'Lord of Karma' as Rudolf Steiner also called Him, that in every detail it is the result of our own thinking, feeling and will intentions from our previous life, so that we can undergo our higher development in total freedom.

The after-death review is the trigger for making a resolution about a new life, a new karmic plan. And the karmic plan is the prerequisite for our further development, which necessarily extends over many lives. We see in Fig. 2 that the after-death review in the spiritual world is connected with a karmic plan for a new, future life ['B'] and that the earlier life plan is based on the review of an earth life that took place previously ['A', see Fig. 3].

Reincarnation and karma are beyond doubt, and they are the result of free, conscious human individuality. Since the awakening of our 'I' at the 'turning-point of time', we began to become master of our lower self, our egotism, through the facility of repeated earth lives and karmic plans, and thus began to lead ourselves and the earth to a higher state of existence.

Since we do not act in life like a perfected Bodhisattva,* the need for another life and – in light of all-pervading goodness – also the *desire* for a further life, exist.

It is not so difficult to understand this logical 'spiritual mechanism' of development, of the human being and the human organism. For it is not uncommon for other circumstances to come to one's aid, i.e. the feeling of having

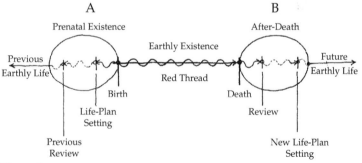

Figure 3

---

*In Buddhist teaching, Bodhisattvas are enlightened beings who have postponed entering paradise in order to help others attain enlightenment. Renouncing their own salvation and immediate entrance into *nirvana*, they devote all their power and energy to saving suffering beings in this world.

experienced something before (*déjà vu*). Many people – probably all – have had this feeling, whether they have heard about reincarnation or not.

I don't want to elaborate much on this aspect – just to give an indication. Have you perhaps ever had the feeling when arriving at a place that you have been there before, even though it is actually quite unknown to you? Have you ever felt exceptionally drawn to a particular place, a time, an era or a literary movement or genre? Or, have you ever had the feeling upon meeting someone that you already know them, even though you have never met before? Certain sympathies and certain antipathies are all signs of a past life. The question of genetics can also be better understood against this background. It is the spirit that is the first and last causal principle, not matter. It is the individuality in the prenatal stage that creates the corresponding body that enables one's life task to be fulfilled successfully.

Mozart did not arise from nothing as a genius of musical composition simply because he inherited the ability for it. Rather, the individuality who later became Wolfgang Amadeus Mozart needed the genes for the achievement of his life plan, and these were to be found in the Mozart family. This is also true in the case of a person that suffers from a particular illness. At first, one may have the feeling that it is unfair if a person has a certain illness, perhaps even from birth. But under certain circumstances, it is for that person (or, as already shown, for that person's relatives) the optimal karmic situation to acquire experiences that they never had before. Often, when people are confronted by a difficult chronic illness, they grow beyond themselves. It also doesn't necessarily depend on whether you conquer an illness, but on what you do with the situation of being ill, what insights or game-changing constellations of destiny result from it.

A current example. Perhaps you have heard that the former German Foreign Minister and Vice Chancellor, Guido Westerwelle, has written a book about his destiny with acute leukemia from which he suffered a year-and-a-half ago. He speaks openly about how he fought his 'demons' through this illness, and how he came to realize what is really necessary for the mission of the earth. Through his illness, he came to experience what is truly essential in life: *love*. It seems as though the illness indicates a karmic cause in relation to Guido Westerwelle's actual life task. The lively words, the somewhat colourful, sometimes provocative demeanour of a well-known politician, may be the reason that now – when he has something important to say (namely something transcendent about death) – people are ready to listen. So, the essential thing is not his political office, and only indirectly the illness. The essential thing is that such insights matured in him, and that very many people are encouraged to have spiritual thoughts due to the fact that he speaks or writes about these insights.

*

Nowadays, many people aspire to a long life, but nobody ultimately wants to grow old in the process. That is an absurd situation. Whoever considers reincarnation seriously, doesn't worry so much about growing old or the length of their lives. This question doesn't burden them, and they have no fear of death. In reality, they have the feeling that it is actually quite good that the body is discarded now and then. For in a single body, in a single context of destiny into which one is born, it is impossible to gather all the experiences the soul needs to perfect itself.

If one is categorically opposed to the immigration of refugees, to take another current example, if one is unable or unwilling to have empathy, to feel compassion, or simply to see that it makes sense to flee from one's own country in order to provide one's self and family freedom from constant bombing, persecution and rape – then at some point that person will need to be reborn in a body, or a constellation of destiny, in which they have a comparable experience, so that they might develop empathy and understanding as a treasure within their soul.

By the way, in most cases the human body loses its life forces once the 'I' has fulfilled its life task, or when there is no longer any prospect that it will do so.

*

In closing, I would like to add that karma, as understood in the Christian-anthroposophical sense, is not bound by 'predestination'. It is entirely up to the individual to decide whether he or she will follow the life plan they made before they were born, and if so, how they will implement it. If it is indeed the human being's mission to gradually develop into an entity that advances in the sense of higher morals – who at some point will even become physically spiritualized, and becomes ever more independent of material surroundings – then it cannot be otherwise. At every moment of life, it is possible for us – with 'moral imagination', as Rudolf Steiner called it – to circumvent our previously determined karmic situation. We are always free within our prenatally designed life plan. If everything were predestined, the human being would never become a responsible being, able in freedom to decide for the good and the true. And finally, it is *we ourselves*, our wise 'eternally living', spirit-conscious 'I', who makes the choice, in the prenatal stage, as well as during earthly life.

This freedom is directly related to the Christ event. You cannot even think of Christianity – it loses its meaning – without consideration of the fact of reincarnation. Why? The central aspect of Christianity is the Resurrection. But what is this Resurrection? We touched on it earlier. Resurrection is actually the chance for individual higher development. It is the awakening after death, the continuation of consciousness after death, and, through that, the ability to set a karmic plan in the light of objectivity and truth – which offers the soul the opportunity to act in the sense of its higher development in the next incarnation.

This way of understanding reincarnation and karma constitutes the greatest difference between the Christian and Buddhist perspectives. This difference also makes it understandable that, according to the Christian understanding, the human being will not reincarnate as an animal – be it an ant or ape! For the meaning of reincarnation is that our soul, our whole being, develops to a higher stage, from life to life – that it gathers experiences so that it will gradually become a divine human being.

This is related to the Christ. And it is also why those who have had near-death experiences report that the spiritual entity that appears to them in the form of love, warmth and light, opened their eyes to their higher purpose.

This Christ-being allows us to recognize our karma, at least in its basic features, through a near-death experience, the postmortem review, or – what is to be striven for, in order to use life effectively in the sense of higher principles – through an inner encounter with the Christ-being in meditation during earthly life. The Christ lets us develop understanding for the constellations of fate in which we sometimes feel trapped. He shows us solutions to hopeless-seeming situations.

Even if recognition of the fact of reincarnation is not yet knowledge of karma in the strict sense, it is the prerequisite for decoding one's own karma. Through the Christian understanding of karma, we can become aware that our personal destiny always stands in conjunction with the destinies of souls linked with us for karmic reasons – even with the whole human soul fraternity. This understanding leads us to the appreciation of the other's destiny, and it frees us from the frightening delusion of being alone. We have the opportunity for higher development through karmic relationships with other people!

When we develop such thoughts, we come with our 'I' into contact with the 'I' of all 'I's – the Christ. For this great 'I' works in our 'I' in the midst of our earthly life.

What affects people deeply who have had near-death experiences and causes them to change their lives so completely, is the acceptance after death of their own sacrosanct individuality by the being of Christ. It affects them so deeply because they know that they are wanted and loved as an eternal individuality. And that is the essential basis for having the courage, despite repeated failures and struggles against their own shortcomings, to follow higher moral principles – also to make sacrifices – in order not only to advance themselves, but humanity as a whole.

Developing a conscious relationship to the spiritual world, namely through the thoughts of reincarnation and karma, is an essential – actually the most essential – act of our life. It is, so to speak, an act of knowledge that paves the way for a truly meaningful way of life.

That is what anthroposophy wishes to call attention to: that there are ways and means of gaining a conscious knowledge of the meaning of one's life today, without waiting for death – without having to hope for a near-death experience. There are ways and means of achieving higher knowledge during earthly life – yes, it is our mission to do this! It is the reason God became human.

A growing understanding of the higher laws of reincarnation and karma places us in the fortunate position of shaping our own destinies consciously and as free spirits, without feeling the straitjacket of predestination. This is a gift of the Christ-being, that the human being can embrace today. And in this way, we will come – to a certain extent – to God's side. This is what Novalis* said in aphoristic words about God and our future humanity: 'God wants gods'. Gradually, we will become world-responsible, creative beings with an eternal consciousness of divine principles, which we freely accept as our own and seek to realize on earth.

---

*Georg Philipp Friedrich Freiherr von Hardenberg (2 May 1772 – 25 March 1801), better known by his pen name Novalis, was an eighteenth-century German aristocrat, poet, author, mystic and philosopher of Early German Romanticism.

APPENDIX 1

From a lecture given to a private audience
on 7 December 2016

A year after her public lecture in Basel, Judith von Halle was
invited to give a private lecture for members of the Para-
celsus Branch of the Anthroposophical Society, entitled 'The
First Hours After death'. As similar themes were discussed, the
closing words of that lecture have been included here:

And finally, I would like to suggest to your hearts a
meditation which, if you so wish, can prepare you for the
night, when it is quieter outside and your souls are preparing
to enter the spiritual world. It is for good reason that it is
said that sleep is 'the little brother of death'. It is a simple
thought, but – and you will feel this if you do it correctly – it
is a thought that touches upon the central event of human
development, thus the all-important, decisive thought that
enables us to take our higher ideals seriously.

For this reason, this little meditation – which you need
to practise with a kind of childlike devotion if you wish
to be lastingly transformed by it – seems to me to be also
suitable for people well-versed in anthroposophy, and
especially for those who consider themselves enlightened
anthroposophical thinkers. For anthroposophical thinking
is really not possible without the intimate, heartfelt inter-
nalization of the facts that make up the content of this meditation. The more 'knowledge' one accumulates, the harder
it is to develop the basic mood – which I have described

as a kind of childlike devotion – and thus ultimately the prerequisite for a true anthroposophical way of thinking.

Consider for a moment the following thoughts. As humanity, we have come to the deepest point of our development, in that we have completely united ourselves with material existence. At this point, we no longer have a relationship to the living spirit, to spiritual reality, from a purely natural predisposition. When we are born into the world, such a natural awareness of spiritual reality is no longer present. We walk the earth and the material world, which we perceive with our senses, appears before our consciousness. But we have no awareness of *spiritual* life.

Without awareness of spiritual life, we must consider ourselves just as mortal and transitory as all other objects in the material, sensory world. So, at this point in our human development we are (metaphorically speaking) caught in a swamp, unable to breathe, unable to stand up on our own. Firstly, this is a thought that has to take shape in the soul, the fatalistic aspect of which one has to bring to one's unadorned consciousness: By ourselves, we are unable to free ourselves from this situation!

What happens at this point? The inconceivable happens. Something which cannot be grasped with ordinary understanding. God Himself – the creator of the world, the creator of all creatures – has so much love and compassion for us that He sends his only Son, the crown of his heart, to the earth – and lets Him suffer an ignominious death for the loosening of our chains, which we had ultimately put on ourselves. There is probably no more ignominious death that a being can suffer than the one that this God suffered, humbling and degrading Himself for our sake, to help us out of the morass.

What we feel about this should not be some kind of medieval, artificially created self-abasement, but rather a natural feeling of shame, springing intuitively from a sincere heart, at the very thought of this sacrifice of love that the Creator of the world made for us. As a consequence, holy humility grows within us, and the question: 'What can I do to thank God for this incredible deed? What can I do to show my thanks that, through His sacrifice, He gave me the means to raise myself out of the morass?'

Anyone who can place the significance of God's sacrifice before their soul, will immediately feel the urgent need to make it apparent to the Godhead that they do not overlook this sacrifice of love, but rather show their gratitude for it.

So what can you do to thank God for His love? Is it at all possible? I think that we can do something. Every one of us can make an effort to use the potential that He fought for – to tap into that reservoir of strength, to reconnect to the spiritual world, and in this way attempt to raise ourselves out of the muddy swamp. We can – thanks to His sacrificial act – muster the strength and focus our will in such a way that we overcome our lower selfhood, our selfishness. For that is the muddy swamp in which we are caught.

If we don't use this reservoir of strength, then – as Rudolf Steiner repeatedly warned – Christ will have died for nothing, and the Mystery of Golgotha will have happened for nothing.

You know the words from the Gospel of John of the so-called 'farewell address' of Christ Jesus: *'No one has greater love than this, that he lay down his life for his friends. […] I no longer call you servants, because the servant knows not what the master is doing. I have called you friends, for I have made known to you everything that I have heard from my Father* (John 15:13).

Yes, my dear present company, if we who recognize God's sacrifice as our salvation are called *'friends'* by Him, then we *know* what the Son made known to us from the Father, namely: *'This is my commandment: that you love one another as I have loved you* (John 15:12). And *how* did He love us? He loved us *selflessly.*

Thankfully, Rudolf Steiner draws attention to the fact that God himself had no need to do this deed, and that we owe this decision to God's self-sacrifice in order for us to become 'free beings'. 'Only then is the thought of freedom justified.'*

But what do we use this freedom for, which God has bought so dearly by His sacrifice of love? For our freedom to decide to love one another, as He has loved us!

When, especially, we have anthroposophical concepts to hand, and thus a deeper understanding of the world's interrelationships, we stand before a great challenge, a great responsibility. We, of all people, know very well what needs to be done, but don't necessarily act accordingly and with the required emphasis.

---

*'For the fact that we can be free beings we have to thank a Divine Act of Love. As human beings we may feel as free beings, but we may never forget that for this freedom we must thank this Act of Love. Then, in the midst of our feeling, the thought will arise: 'You can attain to the value, the dignity, of a human being; but one thing you may not forget, that for being what you are you have to thank Him who has brought back to you your human prototype through the Redemption on Golgotha.' We should not be able to think of freedom without thinking of Redemption through Christ. Only then is the thought of freedom justified. If we will to be free, we must bring the offering of thanks to Christ for our freedom. Only then can we really perceive it.' Quoted from From Rudolf Steiner, *From Jesus to Christ*, Lecture 10, 14 October 1911, p. 182 (Rudolf Steiner Press, 1991).

The Gospel of John goes on to say: *'If I had not come and spoken to them, they would have had no sin. But now they have no excuse for their sin. [...] But now they have seen [my works] and have hated me as well as my father'* (John 15: 22-24). If I do not do and implement what I know is right, then it means hating both the Christ and the Father.

We should not always point our finger at others. One should also take oneself to task. I should be able to admit to myself: Yes, this hatred of the Son and the Father would probably be the result of accepting and using anthroposophical concepts, taken from anthroposophical spiritual science, *without my heart!*

In his penultimate so-called 'guiding principle' – the final thoughts that Rudolf Steiner wrote down (in March 1925) as a kind of legacy* – he states that even the ideas of Hegel, Schelling or Fichte have no spiritual content. Instead, as Rudolf Steiner writes, '... they presented spiritless ideas as the creative world content'.† Just imagine!

---

*See Rudolf Steiner, *Anthroposophical Leading Thoughts, Anthroposophy as a Path of Knowledge, The Michael Mystery* (Rudolf Steiner Press, 1998).

†'Thinkers lost the spiritual content in their ideas. In the idealism of the first half of the nineteenth century they presented spiritless ideas as the creative world content – Fichte, Schelling, Hegel, for example; or they pointed to something supersensible which evaporates because it is bereft of spirit – Spencer, John Stuart Mill and others. Ideas are dead when they do not seek the living spirit. The spiritual vision for the spiritual was now lost. A 'continuation' of the old spiritual knowledge is not possible. The human soul forces, with the consciousness soul unfolding in them, must strive for a renewed elementary and directly living union with the spirit-world. Anthroposophy wishes to be this striving.' From Rudolf Steiner's essay 'Historical Cataclysms at the Dawn of the Spiritual Soul', March 1925, *Anthroposophical Leading Thoughts* (translator's rendering).

So, why are these ideas worthless? Because they are not related to reality! And I can't come close to reality, even with the cleverest, shrewdest thinking, if I don't bring it to life through love and selflessness. Christ, God, needs a dwelling-place on earth in order to be able to work here. And this dwelling-place is not our brain. It is our heart.

In conclusion, I would therefore like to appeal especially to the 'knowledgeable' anthroposophists among us. How many people living on earth are privileged enough to have an understanding, founded on spiritual science, of the human being and the world's interrelationships?! Specifically, for this small group of people, it is important to persevere in the matter of the heart, and not to become indifferent to compassion, selflessness and love as a consequence of this advanced understanding. For if – as predicted in the Apocalypse of John – there will only be a few who will save their brothers and sisters, then only those can belong to these few who, in addition to their understanding and knowledge, also have the will to make sacrifices – the willingness to keep the commandment of Christ and to love their brothers and sisters as they themselves are loved by Christ: selflessly.

If this little meditation, this thought, unfolds in our souls with the vitality that grasping this thought has in spiritual reality, then one can truly speak of an *awakening* – then we will change our lives from the ground up, align with love from the ground up. We become new. This is the overcoming of egoism, of selfishness.

So, dear friends, let us not delay! Let us become friends of God for the sake of our fellow human beings and ourselves!

APPENDIX 2

An extract from George Ritchie's Return from Tomorrow

For now I saw that it was not light but a Man who had entered the room, or rather, a Man made out of light, though this seemed no more possible to my mind than the incredible intensity of the brightness that made up His form. The instant I perceived Him, a command formed itself in my mind. 'Stand up!' The words came from inside me, yet they had an authority my mere thoughts had never had. I got to my feet, and as I did came the stupendous certainty: 'You are in the presence of *the* Son of God.'*

Every detail of twenty years of living was there to be looked at. The good, the bad, the high points, the run-of-the mill. And with this all-inclusive view came a question. It was implicit in every scene and, like the scenes themselves, seemed to proceed from the living Light beside me. *What did you do with your life?*

It was obviously not a question in the sense that He was seeking information, for what I had done with my life was in plain view. In any case this total recalling, detailed and perfect, came from Him, not me. I could not have remembered a tenth of what was there until He showed it to me. *What did you do with your life?*

It seemed to be a question about values, not facts: what did you accomplish with the precious time you were

---

*Quoted from George Ritchie with Elizabeth Sherrill, *Return from Tomorrow*, pages 48-49 (Kingsway Publications, 1978).

allotted? And with this question shining through them, these ordinary events of a fairly typical boyhood seemed not merely unexciting, but trivial. Hadn't I done anything lasting, anything important? Desperately I looked around me for something that would seem worthwhile in the light of this blazing Reality.*

Hadn't I ever gone beyond my own immediate interests, done anything other people would recognize as valuable? At last I located it, the proudest moment of my life:

'I became an Eagle Scout!'

Again, words seemed to emanate from the Presence beside me:

That glorified you.

It was true. I could see myself standing in the center of the award circle, flushed with pride, the admiring eyes of my family and friends turned on me. Me, me, me – always in the center. Wasn't there any time in my life when I had let someone else stand there?[†]

What have you done with your life to show Me?

Already I understood that in my first frantic efforts to come up with an impressive answer, I had missed the point altogether. He was not asking about accomplishment and awards.

The question, like everything else proceeding from Him, had to do with love. How much have you loved with your life? Have you loved others as I am loving you? Totally, Unconditionally?

Hearing the question like that, I saw how foolish it was even to try to find an answer in the scenes around us. Why,

---

*Page 52.
[†]Page 53.

I had not known love like this was possible. Someone should have told me, I thought indignantly! [...]

But though these thoughts rose out of self-pity and self-excuse, the answering thought held no rebuke, only that hint of heavenly laughter behind the words:

I did tell you.

But how? Still wanting to justify myself. How could He have told me and I not have heard?

I told you by the life I lived. I told you by the death I died. And if you keep your eyes on Me, you will see more...*

---

*Pages 54-55.

Books to challenge  *your perception of reality*

A message from Clairview

We are an independent publishing company with a focus on cutting-edge, non-fiction books. Our innovative list covers current affairs and politics, health, the arts, history, science and spirituality. But regardless of subject, our books have a common link: they all question conventional thinking, dogmas and received wisdom.

Despite being a small company, our list features some big names, such as Booker Prize winner Ben Okri, literary giant Gore Vidal, world leader Mikhail Gorbachev, modern artist Joseph Beuys and natural childbirth pioneer Michel Odent.

So, check out our full catalogue online at
www.clairviewbooks.com
and join our emailing list for news on new titles.

office@clairviewbooks.com

CLAIRVIEW